I0105848

Publishing Isn't Marketing Companion Workbook

Is Your Novel "Just Another Can Of Beans" On The Shelf?

Mark Wilder

Wilder Creek Publishing

Copyright © 2025 by Mark Wilder
All rights reserved.

This workbook is a companion volume to *Publishing Isn't Marketing* and contains original guided content, frameworks, and implementation material developed to expand on the core marketing systems introduced in the primary text. While it references the original title, it constitutes a separate work for copyright and cataloging purposes.

No portion of this publication may be reproduced, stored in a retrieval system, or transmitted in any form or by any means—electronic, mechanical, photocopying, recording, or otherwise—without prior written permission, except for brief quotations in reviews or educational settings permitted by law.

For permission requests, contact:
Wilder Creek Publishing
30 N Gould Street Suite 29208
Sheridan, WY 82801

ISBN: 978-1-970587-19-7 (Paperback Workbook)
Library of Congress Control Number: 2025928248
Cover design and illustration assembled using Canva Pro.
Final cover copyright © 2025 by Mark Wilder
Interior layout using Atticus

Published by Wilder Creek Publishing
Sheridan, Wyoming
www.WilderCreekPublishing.com

This book is part of the series:
The Wilder Way to Getting Things Done — Reference Books to Improve Your Life
Companion Title: Publishing Isn't Marketing (Primary Guide)
MarkWilderAuthor.com
First Printed in Sheridan, Wyoming, United States of America
First Edition: December 2025
10 9 8 7 6 5 4 3 2 1

The Wilder Way to Get Things Done

Reference Books to Improve Your Life

*T*HE *WILDER WAY TO Get Things Done* is a growing reference series designed to explain the systems that quietly determine success in modern life—and to make those systems usable by people who were never taught how they work.

Each book in the series focuses on a specific domain where outcomes are often misunderstood, obscured, or oversimplified: how careers advance, how projects actually get finished, how money, marketing, time, technology, or institutions really function behind the scenes. Rather than offering motivation or shortcuts, the series breaks complex processes down into clear structures, practical decisions, and repeatable frameworks.

These books are written for intelligent, capable people who are willing to do the work—but who have not been given a map. People who sense that effort alone is not enough, and that results depend on understanding the rules of the system you are operating within.

The goal of the series is not to tell readers what to think, but to show them how things work. Each volume emphasizes clarity over hype, explanation over opinion, and execution over theory. The tone is grounded, direct, and realistic—designed to leave readers more capable, more confident, and better equipped to make informed decisions in areas that affect their careers and lives.

The Wilder Way is not about perfection, hustle culture, or overnight success. It is about competence, leverage, and long-term sustainability. Build the foundation once. Refine it over time. Use it wherever it applies.

Each volume stands on its own. Together, they form a practical library for people who want to understand the systems around them—and use that understanding to move forward with purpose.

Why This Workbook Exists

W HEN AN AUTHOR PUBLISHES their first book, they often believe the hardest part is over. They wrote it. They edited it. They pressed "publish." They expect momentum to begin naturally.

What they discover instead is silence.
Not failure — silence.
Not rejection — invisibility.
This workbook exists to eliminate that silence.

Publishing Isn't Marketing was written to reveal why most self-published books disappear and how to build a marketing system capable of making a book truly discoverable. This companion workbook turns that system into action. It is not theory, not encouragement, and not a motivational journal. It is a set of guided steps, structured prompts, and planning matrices designed to move an author from "hope" to "execution."

In these pages, you will create:
A professional author identity and digital headquarters
A metadata and ISBN structure that prevents discoverability failure
A search-and-AI footprint that teaches the internet how to find your book
A social presence designed for longevity instead of exhaustion
A bookstore and library plan based on professional standards
An ARC and review pipeline that builds credibility before launch day
A 90-day launch framework that turns a book into a business asset
You will not complete this workbook in one sitting — nor should you.

Books are built in drafts. So are careers.

This workbook was created because too many self-publishing authors are unknowingly set up to fail before they even start.

The pitfalls are not explained.
The systems are not taught.
The industry terminology is never translated into plain language.
The author is left to navigate ISBN conflicts, metadata breakdowns, retailer silos, and ad platforms designed to consume budgets rather than build visibility.

The companion guide you now hold is the countermeasure to that landscape.

Use it slowly. Use it deliberately. Use it with the understanding that each page moves you toward something larger than sales: control. Control of your book. Control of your platform. Control of your future releases.

How to Use This Book:

Publishing is the act of making a book available.

Marketing is the act of ensuring it is seen and is not soon forgotten.

This workbook is where you build that difference.

— Mark Wilder
Founder, Wilder Creek Publishing

How To Use This Workbook

THIS WORKBOOK IS NOT a journal, a planner, or a place for casual brainstorming. It is a structured implementation tool designed to turn *Publishing Isn't Marketing* into a working system you can execute.

Every page you complete moves your book closer to discoverability.

Every section you finish reduces future friction.

Every checklist, prompt, and action plan prevents the most common failures in self-publishing.

This workbook is not about motivation — it is about movement.

Before You Begin

You will get the most value from this workbook if:

Your manuscript is complete or in late editing

Your cover design is at least in draft form

You have chosen print and digital formats

You are prepared to select or assign ISBNs

You understand that retail upload is *not* the final step — it is the midpoint

If you are earlier in the writing process, you may still proceed, but treat these pages as preparation rather than action.

How This Workbook Is Structured

Each chapter mirrors a core component of the marketing system outlined in *Publishing Isn't Marketing*.

It will guide you through four phases:

Phase 1 — Foundation

Build the non-negotiables:

Your author platform and digital headquarters

Website structure and purchase pathways

ISBN and edition mapping

Metadata, BISAC, keywords, and catalog identity

Phase 2 — Visibility

Teach the internet how to find you:

SEO and AI-SEO alignment

Backlink strategy and traffic flow

Social platforms selected with intent (not exhaustion)

Search systems, signals, and reinforcement loops

Phase 3 — Credibility

Show readers why your book deserves trust:

ARC planning and execution

Review collection systems

Influencer and micro-influencer integration

Bookstore and library readiness

Phase 4 — Launch & Longevity

Ensure momentum instead of a moment:

Pre-order structure and calendar placement

90-day execution plan

Post-launch follow-ups and retention

Multi-book positioning for long-term presence

How to Complete the Pages

Every chapter will contain three types of pages:

1. Instruction Pages

These explain the *why* and the *how*.

They prevent mistakes that cost visibility, money, and credibility.

2. Action Pages

These tell you exactly what to do next — step by step.

This is where you build the system, not where you think about it.

3. Implementation Worksheets

These convert knowledge into structure:

Checklists

Metadata templates

Chapter-by-chapter launch planning

Contact tracking

ARC/Review routing

ISBN & edition mapping

These pages should be written in pen, not pencil.

This is your system. Commit to it.

What This Workbook Will Not Do

This workbook will not:

Sell the book for you

Replace editing or proofreading

Make ads profitable without foundation

Compensate for poor metadata or weak covers

Generate momentum if you skip the steps

Marketing is not magic.
It is structure, discipline, and consistency.

<u>Most of all, do not be in a hurry. Each chapter could, and should, take a day or more to complete as you research what is needed.</u>

Contents

Chapter One

Your Author Website

Build Your Books a Home

Y OUR WEBSITE IS YOUR headquarters. It is the only space you fully own, and every other part of your marketing system will eventually point back to it.

Use this chapter to decide:
– What your website must do
– Which platform you'll build it on
– How readers will experience your "home" the first time they arrive
– How your books will be presented and purchased

Fill these pages out in pen. You can refine later, but you need decisions now so every later step (metadata, SEO, ARC, launch planning) has a stable destination.

Quick Snapshot – Where You Are Now

Do you already have an author website?

If no, come back here after you have the domain and website started on pages 4 and 5.

If yes, what is the current domain

_____

What is the primary book you're focusing on right now? (Title + Genre)

_____

What is your biggest concern about building or fixing your website?

_____

Author Brand & Promise

Step 1 – Clarify Who You Are to Readers

Before you choose colors, banners, or platforms, you need a clear promise to the reader. Your brand is not your logo — it is the memory a reader keeps of you. Complete these prompts to define how your website should feel and what it should immediately communicate.

Core Brand Statement

In one sentence, what kind of author are you?

_____

_____

_____

Emotional Promise

What emotional promise do you make to your reader?
(Example: "Clever, twisty mysteries in real European cities.")

_____

_____

Reader Fit

Who is your ideal reader for this book or series? Be as specific as possible.

_____

_____

_____

_____

Checkpoint:

If someone lands on your homepage for five seconds, your brand statement and emotional promise should be obvious from your headline, imagery, and book presentation. You will use these answers when you write your homepage text later in this chapter.

Domain & Platform Choices

Step 2 – Choose Your Domain and Platform

Your domain and platform are not permanent tattoos, but they are hard to change later without losing momentum. Use this page to decide on a domain that supports your long-term author career, then choose the platform that best fits your technical comfort level.

Most authors use their FirstNameLastName .com or add Author or Books after their name if their name is not an available domain (examples for an Author with the name Elizabeth Cole would be elizabethcole.com or elizabethcolebooks.com).

Domain Ideas

1 _____

2 _____

3 _____

4 _____

5 _____

Final Decision

Chosen Domain (or the three you are committing to research and securing one):

_____

_____

_____

Platform Selection

Which platform will you use for your author website?

☐ WordPress + WooCommerce

☐ Squarespace

☐ Shopify

☐ Other: _____

Why is this the best choice for you right now and do you plan to change the platform later?

_____

_____

_____

_____

_____

Website Structure: The Core Pages

Step 3 – Map Your Pages (Simple Site Structure)

Your first website does not need ten menus and four submenus. Most authors need five core pages:
– *Home*   – *Books*   – *About/Bio*   – *Contact*   – *Store*

Home Page
What should a new reader see and understand immediately?

_____

_____

Books Page
How will you group or present your books (by series, genre, reading order)?

_____

_____

About/Bio Page
What do readers need to know about you to trust you?

_____

_____

Contact Page
How should readers, media, or partners be able to reach you?

_____

_____

Store Page
Will you sell direct, or link to retailers, or both?

_____

_____

Homepage Message & Tagline Drafting

Step 4 – Draft Your Homepage Headline and Tagline

Your homepage must immediately answer two questions:

What do you write?

Why should this reader stay?

Use this page to draft a simple headline and subheadline (tagline) you can later refine.

Headline

Headline (big text at the top of your website — in an H1 format heading text):

Example: "Modern Sherlock-Style Mysteries Across Europe"

What will your Headline be?

_____

_____

Subheadline /Tagline / Support Line

Subheadline/tagline (one sentence about you and your promise — in an H2 format heading text):

Example: "Twisty, character-driven crime novels for readers who love clever puzzles and real-world settings."

What will your subheadline/tagline be?

_____

_____

Call to Action

Primary Call to Action (what you want them to do first):

Example: "Start with The Lisbon Exchange" or "See All Books".

What will your Call to Action be?

_____

_____

Note to Self:

When you build your homepage, this headline + subheadline + call to action will be the core of your hero/header section.

Visual Branding Basics (Colors & Fonts)

Step 5 – Visual Consistency: Colors & Fonts

Your goal is not to become a graphic designer. Your goal is to be recognizable. Use this page to make simple, repeatable choices you can use on your website, bookmarks, and social profiles.

Colors

Choose your Brand Colors (Name + Hex or description if you don't know the code)
Primary Color (buttons, headings):

_____

Secondary Color (accents, links):

_____

Background/Neutral Color:

_____

Fonts

Fonts (or font styles) to use across your website
Heading Font (or style):

_____

Body Text Font:

_____

Keep it simple. Two fonts, used consistently, will look more professional than five fonts used randomly.

Book Data for Website (ISBNs & Formats)

Step 6 – List Your Book Formats and ISBNs

Your website should be the authority on your book's identity. Use this page to map each format to its correct ISBN so your site, metadata, and later marketing all match.

Book Title: _____

ISBNs:

Paperback: _____

Hardcover: _____

eBook: _____

Prices:

Paperback: _____

Hardcover: _____

eBook: _____

Notes (platforms listed, release dates, etc.):

Paperback: _____

Hardcover: _____

eBook: _____

Purchase Flow & QR Code Planning

Step 7 – Decide How Readers Will Buy Your Book

This is where you decide what happens when a reader decides "yes." Are they staying on your site to purchase, or being sent to a retailer? Clarify the path now so every QR code, link, and button sends them to the right place.

As mentioned in the book, this is where you decide if they will become your customers, or Amazon's (Barnes & Noble, Walmanrt, etc).

Primary Purchase Path

When a reader clicks "Buy Now" on your website, where should they go first? Why?

_____

_____

_____

Secondary Options (will you offer Amazon, Barnes & Noble, Kobo, signed copy, etc.)?

_____

_____

_____

QR Codes:

Which page will your in-book QR code point to?

(Example: specific book page, review page, your main store, or all three.)

_____

_____

_____

Later chapters will build your QR strategy, review funnel, and ARC systems around the decisions you make here. Do not leave this blank.

Chapter One Summary & Commitments

Chapter One Summary – Your Website Commitments

Use this page to summarize lock in your decisions. You can refine visuals and wording later, but these commitments give the rest of your marketing plan something solid to attach to. This is where you will find your answers easier.

My author brand in one sentence is:

_____

_____

_____

My chosen domain (or target domain) is:

_____

_____

_____

I am building on this platform because:

_____

_____

_____

My homepage headline will roughly say:

_____

_____

_____

My primary "Buy" path will be:

_____

_____

_____

I will have at least these five pages live before launch:

_Checklist with boxes: Home, Books, About, Contact, Store, Other: _____

- ☐ Home
- ☐ Books
- ☐ About (or Bio)
- ☐ Contact
- ☐ Bookstore
- ☐ Other: _____

When this chapter is fully completed, you will have:

– A clear author identity

– A domain and platform decision

– A basic site map

– Draft homepage messaging

– ISBN and format mapping for your website

– A defined purchase path

This is the foundation. In the next chapters, every bit of traffic you earn will have somewhere meaningful to go.

Chapter Two

SEO, AI-SEO & Backlinks

Be Found on the Internet

Orientation & Purpose

If Chapter One built your home, this chapter builds the roads leading to it. Search engines and AI systems cannot guess who you are or what your book is. They learn it from metadata. They confirm it through consistency. They trust it through backlinks — other places on the internet pointing readers back to you.

These worksheets clarify your genre identity, audience, search language, and where you will earn your first backlinks.

What is the primary search phrase you want readers to find you with?
Example: What are new books like Stephen King?

_____

_____

_____

What is the secondary search phrase you want readers to find you with?

_____

_____

_____

Keyword Brainstorm (Reader Language)

What Are Readers Searching For?

Write like a reader searches. Not academic. Not clever. Plain language queries.

Think: "mystery novel set in Lisbon" — not "a mesmerizing tale of self-discovery."

Reader-Language Keywords:

List 10 potential search phrases which would bring readers to your book (no polishing yet):

_____

_____

_____

_____

_____

_____

_____

_____

_____

_____

Final Keyword Selection

Narrow to Your 5–10 Core Terms

Choose the phrases that match your audience, genre promise, and discoverability.

Final Keyword Set:
Check the box as you choose

☐ _____

☐ _____

☐ _____

☐ _____

☐ _____

☐ _____

☐ _____

☐ _____

☐ _____

☐ _____

These phrases must appear (naturally) on your website, YouTube descriptions, Google Books page, and metadata registrations. They cannot live only on Amazon.

SEO Touchpoints

Where to Use Keywords

Match the places you can realistically update this week. This prevents "learning without doing."

Here are the places to get started

☐ Website homepage headline

☐ Website book pages

☐ Image ALT text on cover graphics

☐ Back cover copy (short pitch)

☐ YouTube video descriptions

☐ Pinterest pins & captions

☐ Google Books Partner Center metadata

☐ Social bios (where appropriate)

Which three will you do first? (be realistic)

_____

_____

_____

AI-SEO Identity

AI Search: What Should Systems Learn About You?

AI systems do not scan the whole internet. They confirm identity through consistency of keywords, ISBN mapping, and genre alignment. Tell them who you are in one sentence.

One-Sentence AI Identity Statement
(Example: What 5 new books are similar to Colllen Hoover books —
"Write this in the way a reader would ask an AI system like ChatGPT or Gemini — not how marketer — would search for your book.")

_____

_____

_____

_____

_____

Which books/authors are you adjacent/comparable to?
(For AI prompting alignment — not to make claims of comparison.)

_____

_____

_____

_____

_____

ISBN/Format Confirmation for Discoverability

ISBNs + SEO Mapping

List your formats so you can copy/paste with confidence. This prevents metadata drift, broken links, and mismatched identities.

Book Title: _____

<u>*ISBNs:*</u>

Paperback: _____

Hardcover: _____

eBook: _____

<u>*First platform it will be uploaded to:*</u>

Paperback: _____

Hardcover: _____

eBook: _____

Backlink Planning (Authority & Trust)

Plan Your First 10 Backlinks

Backlinks are votes of confidence. You need at least 10 planned sources. Do not leave this vague — pick the ones you can secure. See Chapter 2 of Publishing Isn't Marketing to guide this

High Authority Targets (3):

* _____

* _____

* _____

Medium Authority Targets (4):

* _____

* _____

* _____

* _____

Low-Effort / Fast Wins (3):

* _____

* _____

* _____

Backlinks are not favors — they are infrastructure. Treat them that way.

Outreach Script Drafts

Draft Your Outreach Language

Write a short version of how you'll request backlinks or listings. No begging. No hype. Clear, professional language. Take your time with your wording. It shows your authorship.

Generic Request (website/blog/YouTube/genre community):

_____

_____

_____

_____

_____

_____

_____

Specific Ask (library, bookstore, academic, podcast, reviewer):

_____

_____

_____

_____

_____

Chapter Two Summary & Commitments

CHAPTER TWO — READY TO DEPLOY

Check the boxes you are prepared to execute:

☐ 10 reader-language keyword phrases drafted

☐ 5–10 core keywords selected for all platforms

☐ Homepage plan updated with keyword alignment

☐ ISBNs mapped to correct formats for metadata

☐ 10 backlink targets listed and prioritized

☐ Outreach scripts drafted and ready to send

☐ At least 3 actions scheduled (date/time)

The first 3 SEO/AI-SEO actions I will complete this week:

_____

_____

_____

When this page is complete, you are no longer waiting for discoverability — you are building it.

Chapter Three

Social Media

Without The Burnout

Social media is not your marketing foundation — your website is.

Social media is a set of bridges that lead readers to a property you control.

Your objective here is not to "go viral." It is to become findable and consistent.

Most authors burn out because they treat every platform as mandatory. That is a waste of time and energy. You will select one primary platform and one secondary platform, and you will ignore everything else until momentum forms.

Primary Platforms (choose one based on genre + audience):

-TikTok (BookTok): fastest discovery, strongest influence on sales volume.
-Instagram (Bookstagram): visual appeal, reliable relationship building.
-YouTube: search-based traffic, strongest long-term SEO, slower start but durable.

Secondary Platforms (choose one):

Email newsletter (any provider): your audience lives here.
Facebook: legacy contacts and local community.
Reddit: credibility and subject expertise; not a sales tool.

You are not posting for entertainment. You are posting to:
1. Show the book exists.

2. Show the book belongs to a defined reader group.

3. Provide a direct line back to your website.

Your social media profile must contain:

    1. Author name (consistent with ISBN metadata)

    2. One clarity statement: "I write _____ for readers who enjoy _____."

    3. A website link. Not Amazon.

Your social posts are not ads. Your posts are evidence.

Platform Selection

This is where you decide the two platforms which will help most, not which you are most comfortable using.

Primary Platform:

_____

Why this platform aligns with my genre:

_____

Secondary Platform:

_____

Primary purpose (readers / authority / newsletter growth):

_____

_____

_____

Profile Draft:

Author Name (as it appears on ISBN): _____

"I write _____."

"For readers who enjoy _____."

Website link (always): _____

First Three Posts

1. _____

2. _____

3. _____

Posting Rhythm (Define Your Capacity)

Days per week I can post consistently (S, M, T, W, Th, F, S): _____

Minutes per day I can commit: _____

Boundaries (what I will not do): _____

Remember
You are not trying to impress the internet.
You are establishing presence.
Consistency is the product.

Chapter Four

Bookstores & Libraries

Real-World Presence

Digital visibility matters, but physical placement is what creates legitimacy.

A social post may be ignored; a book on a shelf is acknowledged.

A website can be clicked past; a library catalog record stays in the system for years.

This chapter is not about "getting into bookstores."

It is about being orderable, reorderable, and professionally positioned.

Before approaching any bookstore or library, confirm the minimum standards are met:

IngramSpark distribution active

    55% wholesale discount

    Returnable enabled

    ISBNs owned or controlled by you (not free/free-platform ISBNs)

    BISAC codes correctly assigned

    Metadata consistent with your website

A bookstore manager's first question is not,

"Is the writing good?"

It is:

"Can I order it, display it, and return it if necessary?"

Your responsibilities:

Make the book orderable through Ingram.

Provide a one-page sell sheet with ISBN(s), pricing, and terms.

Approach stores *professionally*, not emotionally.

Follow up *without pressure*.

Libraries operate on similar logic but prioritize:

Catalog indexes (LCCN or regional equivalent)

Community relevance

Patron requests by ISBN

Author professionalism

Libraries rarely drive immediate sales. They drive repeat readers.

In Review:

Bookstores = retail visibility.

Libraries = long-tail discovery.

Both = stability.

Readiness Check

(Yes / No)

    IngramSpark listing complete: _____

    Wholesale discount set to 55%: _____

    Returnable enabled: _____

    Consistent ISBNs per edition: _____

    BISAC codes selected: _____

    Metadata matches website: _____

    Professional sell sheet created: _____

    If any line is "No," do not approach yet.

My Sell Sheet Items

Title: _____

ISBN(s): _____

Formats (PB/HC/EB): _____

Wholesale Terms: _____

Genre / BISAC Priority: _____

One-Sentence Positioning Line: _____

_____

_____

First Five Locations to Approach

_____

_____

_____

_____

_____

Script Prep

_____

_____

Follow-up date (4–6 weeks after first visit): _____

You are not asking for permission to belong. You are proving readiness.

Chapter Five

Books Live On Reviews

ARC Strategy, Reviews, and Social Proof

"Credibility is earned before the book goes live."

A N ARC (ADVANCE READER Copy) is not a favor someone does for you — it is a marketing tool with a mission. Before a reader trusts a book, they look for evidence that someone else already has.

This chapter builds that evidence.

Your ARC plan will:
• Seed early reviews before launch
• Build trust signals for buyers and algorithms
• Protect your book from launching into silence
• Give real readers a chance to find typos before strangers do
• Create the first generation of advocates for your career

Think of ARCs as a rehearsal before opening night — the audience is small, but their reaction decides whether the theater fills.

This chapter provides:
• Step-by-step setup
• Email/DM outreach templates
• Expectations scripts for ARC readers
• Review placement instructions
• Worksheets to track progress
• Legal and ethical guardrails

We begin where most authors fail: recruiting the *right* readers.

Build Your ARC Team

ARC readers **should not be**:
• Your mom
• Your friends from high school
• Coworkers afraid to hurt your feelings

ARC readers **should be**:
• Genre readers who actually finish books
• People comfortable leaving reviews
• Readers who like to talk about what they read
• A mix of strangers and distant acquaintances
• Members of genre communities (BookTok, Bookstagram, Reddit, etc.)

Start small:
5–12 readers for your first book.
Enough to matter, not enough to overwhelm.

Build Your Recruitment List

This is the format to build your list. We will create 10 entries:

1st Reader Name:

_____

Where You Found Them (TikTok/FB/Goodreads/etc.):

_____

Genre Match?
(Y/N)
Reliable Reviewer?
(Y/N)
Email / Contact:

_____

2nd Reader Name:

_____

Where You Found Them (TikTok/FB/Goodreads/etc.):

_____

Genre Match?
(Y/N)

Reliable Reviewer?
(Y/N)

Email / Contact:

_____

***

3rd Reader Name:

_____

Where You Found Them (TikTok/FB/Goodreads/etc.):

_____

Genre Match?
(Y/N)

Reliable Reviewer?
(Y/N)

Email / Contact:

_____

***

4th Reader Name:

_____

Where You Found Them (TikTok/FB/Goodreads/etc.):

_____

Genre Match?
(Y/N)

Reliable Reviewer?
(Y/N)

Email / Contact:

_____

5th Reader Name:

_____

Where You Found Them (TikTok/FB/Goodreads/etc.):

_____

Genre Match?
(Y/N)
   Reliable Reviewer?
(Y/N)
   Email / Contact:

_____

***

6th Reader Name:

_____

Where You Found Them (TikTok/FB/Goodreads/etc.):

_____

Genre Match?
(Y/N)
   Reliable Reviewer?
(Y/N)
   Email / Contact:

_____

***

7th Reader Name:

_____

Where You Found Them (TikTok/FB/Goodreads/etc.):

_____

Genre Match?
(Y/N)
   Reliable Reviewer?
(Y/N)
   Email / Contact:

_____

8th Reader Name:

_____

Where You Found Them (TikTok/FB/Goodreads/etc.):

_____

Genre Match?
(Y/N)

Reliable Reviewer?
(Y/N)

Email / Contact:

_____

***

9th Reader Name:

_____

Where You Found Them (TikTok/FB/Goodreads/etc.):

_____

Genre Match?
(Y/N)

Reliable Reviewer?
(Y/N)

Email / Contact:

_____

***

10th Reader Name:

_____

Where You Found Them (TikTok/FB/Goodreads/etc.):

_____

Genre Match?
(Y/N)

Reliable Reviewer?
(Y/N)

Email / Contact:

_____

The ARC Reader Agreement (Simple Language)

This is *not a contract*.
It is an expectations script that protects your time and keeps communication professional.

Use the below Reader Expectations to affirm what you want from the ARC Readers, and what they can expect from you

ARC Reader Expectations

Thank you for reading an advance copy of this book. This version is final and may include small errors that can be fixed before the release date. Your role is to:

Read the book within _____ days
Provide feedback on clarity, pacing, and storyline
Leave an honest review on launch week

Please:
Avoid sharing the file publicly or distributing copies
Contact me privately if there is a concern, confusion, or major issue
Notify me separately of any typos that may have been missed in the editing and proofreading processes

Your honesty helps make this book better.
Your review helps readers decide if the story deserves their time.

This sets your expectations without legal tone.

Outreach Scripts

These are customizable fill-in-the-blank templates.

Initial DM/Email

Subject: ARC Invite — *[Book Title]*

Hi *[Name]*,

I'm preparing for the launch of *[Book Title]* and I'm inviting a small group of early readers who enjoy *[genre: e.g., modern detective mystery / small-town romance / dark fantasy]*.

If you'd like to read an advance copy and leave an honest review during launch week, I'd be glad to have you.

Format options: paperback (author copy mailed) or PDF/ePub.
Timeframe: _____ days to read / review.

If interested, reply with:
Mailing address (or email for digital copy)
Preferred format

Either way, thank you for your time.
  – **[Author Name]**
  – **[Author Email]**

Follow-Up Reminder (Polite, Not Pushy)

Ideally send this two weeks prior to launch week

Hi *[Name]*,

Checking in to see if you're still on track for launch week.

If anything changed, no pressure — I'd rather you enjoy the book than rush it.

Just let me know either way.
– **[Author Name]**
– **[Author Email]**

***

Review Week Message

Ideally send this one day prior to launch week – include the direct link to the book on each review site, to make it easier.

Hi *[Name]*,

Today's the day — reviews go live in the morning!

Here are the locations in order of priority:

My author website review page (preferred)
Goodreads
Amazon

I want to take a moment and personally thank you for taking the time to read my book. It truly means a lot to me.
– **[Author Name]**
– **[Author Email]**

Directing Reviews to the Right Place

This connects to the earlier ISBN/website strategy.

Reviews should appear in this order:

1. Your Author Website (the hub you control)
2. Goodreads (for reader culture)
3. Amazon (for algorithms)
4. Secondary platforms as available

This avoids the mistake of giving Amazon all authority.

Review Tracking Page

1st Reader Name:

_____

Format Sent (Print/PDF/ePub):

_____

Date Sent: _____

Review Left?

(Y/N) Where the reviews were left:

_____

Notes for future ARCs:

_____

***

2nd Reader Name:

_____

Format Sent (Print/PDF/ePub):

_____

Date Sent: _____

Review Left?

(Y/N) Where the reviews were left:

_____

Notes for future ARCs:

_____

***

3rd Reader Name:

_____

Format Sent (Print/PDF/ePub):

_____

Date Sent: _____

Review Left?

(Y/N) Where the reviews were left:

_____

Notes for future ARCs:

_____

***

4th Reader Name:

_____

Format Sent (Print/PDF/ePub):

_____

Date Sent: _____

Review Left?

(Y/N) Where the reviews were left:

_____

Notes for future ARCs:

_____

***

5th Reader Name:

_____

Format Sent (Print/PDF/ePub):

_____

Date Sent: _____

Review Left?

(Y/N) Where the reviews were left:

_____

Notes for future ARCs:

_____

***

6th Reader Name:

_____

Format Sent (Print/PDF/ePub):

_____

Date Sent: _____

Review Left?
(Y/N) Where the reviews were left:

_____

Notes for future ARCs:

_____

***

7th Reader Name:

_____

Format Sent (Print/PDF/ePub):

_____

Date Sent: _____

Review Left?
(Y/N) Where the reviews were left:

_____

Notes for future ARCs:

_____

***

8th Reader Name:

_____

Format Sent (Print/PDF/ePub):

_____

Date Sent: _____

Review Left?
(Y/N) Where the reviews were left:

_____

Notes for future ARCs:

_____

***

9th Reader Name:

_____

Format Sent (Print/PDF/ePub):

_____

Date Sent: _____

Review Left?

(Y/N) Where the reviews were left:

_____

Notes for future ARCs:

_____

***

10th Reader Name:

_____

Format Sent (Print/PDF/ePub):

_____

Date Sent: _____

Review Left?

(Y/N) Where the reviews were left:

_____

Notes for future ARCs:

_____

How ARC Readers Protect You

A strong ARC team prevents:
• Public embarrassment from missed typos
• 1-star reviews about formatting errors
• "No one has read this" buyer hesitation
• Silent launches that look abandoned

They create:
• First social proof
• First search signals
• First SEO/AI recognition
• First bookstore & library trust moments

ARC Readers are not fans — they are the foundation of your launch.

END-OF-CHAPTER CHECKLIST

[ ] 5–12 ARC readers confirmed

[ ] Agreement sent and acknowledged

[ ] Copies delivered

[ ] Review deadlines scheduled

[ ] Reminder messages planned

[ ] Website review page ready (QR code recommended)

[ ] ISBNs displayed and consistent

[ ] Launch week review push prepared

If you cannot check at least 5 boxes, do not launch yet.
Fix the foundation first.

Chapter Six

Metadata, ISBNs & BISAC

Your Book's Digital DNA

T HIS CHAPTER EXISTS FOR one reason:
  Most indie authors ruin their discoverability before their book ever launches.

Not by bad marketing.

Not by lack of effort.

But by mishandling the three things that determine where their book lives in the world:

  ISBNs (identity)

  Metadata (instructions)

  BISAC codes (location)

  If ISBNs are the passport, metadata is the travel record, and BISAC is the fingerprint.

  Once set and distributed, every system—retail, library, wholesaler, AI, search—will rely on those fingerprints to confirm who you are and where you belong.

Get it wrong, and systems assume:

  Your book is something else

  It should be shown to the wrong readers

  It should be shelved in the wrong section

  It does not belong beside the authors you should be compared to

This is why publishers treat BISAC selection like surgery:

slow, precise, consequence-aware.

Authors who rush this step often destroy months — sometimes years — of marketing potential.

Why BISAC Matters Professionally

BISAC codes determine:

    Which shelf a bookstore uses

    Which search categories an ebook appears in

    Which readers receive algorithmic recommendations

    Which librarians consider it worth acquiring

    Which comparable titles AI uses in discovery prompts

Misalignment triggers silent penalties:

    Wrong audience = negative reviews

    Wrong section = low circulation

    Wrong comparables = AI ignores you

BISAC is not "labels."

BISAC is *placement, positioning, and permission*

Why Publishers Do This Slowly

Publishers have staff solely dedicated to extrapolating BISAC Metadata because:

    They study category sales velocity

    They compare competitor placements

    They measure audience expectations

    They check international metadata conflicts

    They confirm BISAC alignment with ISBN databases

    This is not busywork. It's foundational infrastructure.

Because if it is incorect, the marketing can fail with no recourse.

If you feel overwhelmed, that is not a sign to quit—
it is a sign you are taking it seriously enough.

BISAC Decision Point & Consequences (Self-Assessment)

Answer honestly:

If my BISAC choices attract the wrong readers, am I prepared for negative reviews?
Yes / No

If my metadata misaligns, am I willing to lose bookstore/library opportunities?
Yes / No

If I choose BISAC codes too broadly, am I willing to be invisible in algorithmic sorting?
Yes / No

Based on my expertise, should I consider an Author Centric Publisher or metadata consultation?
Yes / No

If more than one "Yes" feels uncomfortable, pause here.
Do not assign BISAC yet.

Draft BISAC Hierarchy

Primary (shelf placement / core promise):

_____

_____

Secondary (algorithmic fit / reader expectation):

_____

_____

Tertiary (niche signal / precision for ideal readers):

_____

_____

Competitor Alignment

List 3 well known authors your readers would also buy books from:

_____

_____

_____

Where are they shelved?

_____

Do you genuinely belong there, with them?

Yes / No

If "No," adjust before proceeding.

Did you choose the same options as them?

Yes / No

If "No," adjust before proceeding.

Before You Lock BISAC

I confirm the following:

[ ] My BISAC hierarchy reflects reader expectation, not my preference

[ ] I understand Primary = shelf, Secondary = algorithm, Tertiary = niche

[ ] I checked competitors in the same section

[ ] I am not mixing codes just to increase exposure

[ ] I am not selecting categories that mislead readers

Signature (Your commitment to accuracy for your readers): _____

This is not admin work. This is identity work.

BISAC is not what your book is.

BISAC is where your book lives.

BISAC CATEGORIES AND INFORMATION

BISAC codes are copyrighted classifications owned by the Book Industry Study Group (BISG). This workbook cannot reproduce the full list, and authors should always reference the official BISG master list for current codes. Most publishing platforms offer partial versions, but the BISG list is the source of truth. Always verify against the BISG listing before submitting metadata or uploading to any platform.

Where to Find BISAC Codes

A complete and current listing of BISAC Subject Headings is maintained by the Book Industry Study Group (BISG).

Visit BISG.org to see the complete listing. Click the "*BISAC*" tab on the menu.

Authors can browse the full catalog of codes directly on the BISG reference page. This is the only authoritative version.

BISAC codes are updated periodically, and individual platforms (Bowker, IngramSpark, KDP, etc.) may display partial or outdated lists.

__Always use the BISG master list as your source of truth before assigning codes.__

Chapter Seven

Influencers, Micro-Influencers, and Ethical Outreach

Not all influencers are created equal. You are not chasing scale; you are pursuing alignment.

Micro Influencers:

Follower Range: 1K–25K

Cost: Free / ARC / low fee

Pros: Highest engagement, best conversions

Cons: Smaller reach

Mid-Tier Influencers:

Follower Range: 25K–100K

Cost: Often paid

Pros: Credibility + measurable results

Cons: Selective, genre-dependent

Major Influencers:

Follower Range: 100K+

Cost: Paid / difficult to access

Pros: Wide reach, cultural momentum

Cons: Low conversion for debut authors

Borrowed trust, without begging for it.

Influencer outreach is not about going viral.

It is not about getting a celebrity endorsement.

It is not about sending hundreds of free copies into a void.

Professional outreach is about aligning with people who already influence your audience's decisions, then giving them what they need to share your book confidently.

Readers trust humans more than headlines.

They trust recommendations more than ads.

They trust people who remind them of themselves.

A single trusted voice can outperform a $500 ad campaign.

Understanding Influencer Tiers

Not all influencers are created equal. You are not chasing scale; you are pursuing alignment.

Micro Influencer

Follower Range: 1K–25K

Cost: Free / ARC / low fee

Pros: Highest engagement, best conversions

Cons: Smaller reach

Mid-Tier Influencer

Follower Range: 25K–100K

Cost: Often paid

Pros: Credibility + measurable results

Cons: Selective, genre-dependent

Major Influencer

Follower Range: 100K+

Cost: Paid / difficult to access

Pros: Wide reach, cultural momentum

Cons: Low conversion for debut authors

Your target for a first or second book: Micro + Mid-tier.
This is where trust lives. This is where readers move.

How to Find the Right Influencers

Your goal is not "big names." Your goal is genre fit + audience trust.

Search by:
• Hashtags #BookTok, #Bookstagram, #BookRec, #MysteryBooks, etc.
• Genre-specific communities (e.g., cozy, thriller, romantasy, etc.)
• Reviewers who talk about books similar to yours
• Creators who are already reading indie or hybrid authors
• Influencers who speak *to* their audience, not *at* them

Avoid:
• Accounts with inflated follower counts and low engagement
• Creators promoting "everything that shows up"

• People who post only sponsored content
• Anyone requesting payment *before* confirming genre alignment

If their audience is not your audience, the number doesn't matter.

Outreach Scripts

Initial Engagement (Before You Ask Anything)

Like 15–25 posts, as you start.

Comment genuinely. Look for genuine responses and dialogue to judge the influencers engaement.

Do not mention your book. yet.

First Contact Message

Hi [*Name*],

I've enjoyed your posts about [specific genre or book]. Your audience seems to appreciate grounded recommendations, and I think my upcoming book may align with what they enjoy.

Would you be open to reviewing an advance reader copy of my new book, *[Title]*, a [short 5–9 word genre identity]?

If not, thank you for what you contribute to the reading community.
If yes, I'll send more details and format options.

Respectfully,
[Author Name]
[Website link]

After They Accept

Hi [*Name*],
Please choose your format options: Print ARC / ePub / PDF
The timeframe, based on my launch schdule: _____ days to read / review
Review Preference: Honest. Not promotional. Your voice matters more than praise.

Respectfully,
[Author Name]
[Website link]

Decline Response

Hi [*Name*],

Thank you for letting me know. If you ever wish to revisit it, I'm here.

Respectfully,
[Author Name]
[Website link]

No pressure. No guilt. No begging.

What Influencers Need From You

Influencers promote books that are:
- Easy to summarize
- Easy to categorize
- Easy to recommend
- Easy to link

They need:
- A short pitch (not the back cover copy)
- A single primary link (your website, NOT Amazon first)
- Visual assets (cover, tagline graphic, optional quote)
- ISBN for metadata alignment
- A deadline that respects their schedule

You are not buying words — you are gaining respectful credibility.

Ethical Compensation

Acceptable:
- Free print copy
- $25–$75 honorarium for time
- Giveaway copy for their audience

Not acceptable:
- Paying for a guaranteed positive review
- Requesting certain star ratings
- Penalizing a negative review
- Controlling tone or message

Payment compensates the labor — not the verdict.

Your target for a first or second book: Micro + Mid-tier.
This is where trust lives. This is where readers move.

How to Find the Right Influencers

Your goal is not "big names." Your goal is genre fit + audience trust.

Search by:
- Hashtags #BookTok, #Bookstagram, #BookRec, #MysteryBooks, etc.
- Genre-specific communities (e.g., cozy, thriller, romantasy, etc.)
- Reviewers who talk about books similar to yours
- Creators who are already reading indie or hybrid authors
- Influencers who speak *to* their audience, not *at* them

Avoid:
- Accounts with inflated follower counts and low engagement
- Creators promoting "everything that shows up"
- People who post only sponsored content
- Anyone requesting payment *before* confirming genre alignment

If their audience is not your audience, the number doesn't matter.

Outreach Scripts

Use these to help format the messages and iteraction with influencers

Initial Engagement (Before You Ask Anything)
Like 8–10 posts.

Comment genuinely, and often, over a two week period.

Gauge their interaction with your comments.

Do not mention your book yet

First Contact Message
Hi [*Name*],

I've enjoyed your posts about [specific genre or book]. Your audience seems to appreciate grounded recommendations, and I think my upcoming book may align with what they enjoy.

Would you be open to reviewing an advance reader copy of my new book, *[Title]*, a [short 5–9 word genre identity]?

If not, thank you for what you contribute to the reading community.

If yes, I'll send more details and format options.

Respectfully,
[Author Name]
[Website link]

After They Accept
Hi [*Name*],

Format options: Print ARC / ePub / PDF
Timeframe: _____ days to read / review
Review Preference: Honest. Not promotional. Your voice matters more than praise.

Respectfully,
[Author Name]
[Website link]

Decline Response
Hi [*Name*],

Thank you for letting me know. If you ever wish to revisit it, I'm here.

Respectfully,
[Author Name]
[Website link]

No pressure. No guilt. No begging.

What Influencers Need From You

Influencers promote books that are:
- Easy to summarize
- Easy to categorize
- Easy to recommend
- Easy to link

They need:
- A short pitch (not the back cover copy)
- A single primary link (your website, NOT Amazon first)
- Visual assets (cover, tagline graphic, optional quote)
- ISBN for metadata alignment
- A deadline that respects their schedule

You are not buying words — you are raising credibility

Ethical Compensation

Acceptable:
- Free print copy
- $25–$75 honorarium for time
- Giveaway copy for their audience

Not acceptable:
- Paying for a guaranteed positive review
- Requesting certain star ratings
- Penalizing a negative review
- Controlling tone or message

Payment compensates the labor — not the verdict

Tracking System

Influencer Name: _____

Platform: _____

Follower Count: _____

Contact Sent: _____

ARC Sent: _____

Review Confirmed: _____

Link Received: _____

Notes: _____

***

Influencer Name: _____

Platform: _____

Follower Count: _____

Contact Sent: _____

ARC Sent: _____

Review Confirmed: _____

Link Received: _____

Notes: _____

***

Influencer Name: _____

Platform: _____

Follower Count: _____

Contact Sent: _____

ARC Sent: _____

Review Confirmed: _____

Link Received: _____

Notes: _____

Chapter Eight

Converting Attention Into Readers

Making Your Website Work For You

Where traffic becomes trust, and trust becomes revenue.

Your website is not decoration.
It is not an optional extra.
It is the operational center of your author career.

Social media creates interest.
Influencers create conversation.
ARCs create credibility.

But none of those matter if there is nowhere to send the reader.

A professional author website converts curiosity into action — and that action is where careers are built:
• Purchasing the book
• Joining a newsletter
• Exploring your series
• Requesting event information
• Leaving a review

Without a website, all momentum leaks back into the platforms, not into your career.

With a website, momentum compounds.

The Three Website Pages That Must Be Built Up Now

You have made your website at the start of this workbook. We will not make it work for you.

The Home Page — First Impression

Purpose:
• Tell visitors who you are, what you write, and why they should care.

Required elements to add:
• Book cover(s) at the top
• 8–12 word positioning statement (genre identity)
• 1 link to the bookstore section
• 1 link to newsletter sign-up

You can build in three Calls to Action which guide the visitors to your website:
[ ] Shop The Bookstore
[ ] Download Free First Chapters
[ ] Join the Newsletter for Updates

Joining the newsletter makes the visitor your reader, or future reader, and becomes a customer for the life of your books.

The Book Page In The BookStoore — Where Curiosity Becomes Commitment

Purpose:
• Provide clarity, not pressure.

Minimum required:
• Cover image
• Back-cover blurb or long description
• ISBNs for every edition
• Buy buttons (to your website's shopping cart, never to a retailer's platform)

Checklist for You to Build:
[ ] Paperback ISBN here: _____
[ ] Ebook ISBN here: _____
[ ] Hardcover ISBN (if applicable): _____
[ ] Links to other books in the series (if applicable): _____

The Book Review Hub — Where Trust Lives On The Book Page

This is where you place:
• Review submission form
• Links to external reviews
• Quotes from early ARC readers
• A subscribe button (YES — also place it right here)

Loved this book? Leave a review here — it matters more than you know.

<*Submit Review On Book*>

(on your book's page)

After submitting, please choose any of these platform below to share it with other readers.

Build these buttons under it:

- Goodreads
- Barnes & Noble
- Kobo
- Google Books
- Amazon

And immediately underneath:

Want updates, early chapters, or ARC invitations?

<*Subscribe here before you go*>

QR Codes: Where They Belong

QR codes should never feel random. They are doors, not decorations.

Minimum placements:
- Inside back cover of paperback
- End of ebook
- On your website's book page
- In your ARC materials (if applicable)

3 QR Code Standard Destinations:
→ Your Website's Book Page (NOT Amazon) with the Review Hub
Place at the end of the final chapter
→ Your Website's Bookstore
Place in the Also By section in your back matter
→ Your Next Book Release
Place after the read ahead excerpt of the next book to release

Recommended text under the QR code (copy this):

Books Live On Reviews. Please Review This Book.

OR

Subscribe To Be Notified Of The Release Date

OR

See All Books Written By (Your Name or Pen Name)

EXAMPLE:

Visit Here To Buy Or Review The Guide Book This Companion Goes With:

Light Technical Setup (No Deep Diving)

This workbook is not a WordPress manual, but the following structure prevents broken builds:

Platform Recommendations:

• WordPress + Elementor + WooCommerce → most control

• Squarespace → simplest setup, less scalable

• Shopify → good for merch-heavy authors, higher cost

• Wix → last resort; SEO limitations

You are not choosing a theme.

You are choosing autonomy.

Technical Non-Negotiables:

[ ] SSL certificate active (https)

[ ] Load time under 3 seconds

[ ] Mobile layout tested

[ ] Secure checkout connected

[ ] Bookstore page functional BEFORE launch

Hybrid Marketing Flow

This diagram is in the workbook as a reference:

Reader sees influencer → clicks link → website home page

↓

Home page clarifies identity → clicks book page

↓

Book page offers purchase → chooses your store or retailer

↓

Checkout email → auto triggers newsletter invite

↓

Newsletter → builds long-term reader relationship

↓

Future releases → repeat without rebuilding the system

This is how marketing stops from feeling like constant reinvention.

End-of-Chapter Confirmation

You are ready to move forward when:

[ ] My website has a homepage, book page, and review hub

[ ] All ISBNs are visible in one central location

[ ] A QR code leads to my website, not a retailer

[ ] My store can accept payments

[ ] My site is ready before I ask anyone to look at it

If fewer than four are checked: *stop. stabilize. build. then continue.*

Chapter Nine

Reader to Retention

A Repeatable System that Builds a Career

Publishing a book is a single moment.
Building a readership is a system.

This chapter turns the work you have already done into an operating pipeline — one that takes a reader from interest, to review, to subscription, to preorder, to lifelong reader.

By now, you have:
• A professional website (your headquarters)
• ISBN and metadata alignment (your identity)
• SEO/AI-SEO pathways (your map)
• Social platforms pointing inward (your bridges)

This chapter activates the next phase — the one most authors skip:
Retention.

Because a launch grows a moment.
A system grows a career.

The Pipeline That Replaces Guesswork

This is the chapter's backbone. Every action in Chapters 2–8 feeds into this:

Reader → Review Button → Website → Subscribe → Preorder → Return Reader

Written as a process:
Reader finishes → sent to a Review Hub on your website, not a retail site first
Review leaves a footprint where YOU own the data
Reader is invited to subscribe before leaving
Subscriber is invited to preorder the next title or join early-access
Retention loop repeats for the next release

This is how a reader becomes an audience.
This is how an audience makes this your career.

The Author Career View

Here's the shift that ends burnout:
Most authors market as if each book is an isolated event.
Professionals market as if each book is a brick — building a structure they intend to live in.

The model:
Book 1 = Proof of Concept
Book 2 = Credibility
Book 3 = Career
Book 4+ = Catalog Power

When libraries reorder your series without being asked?
When bookstores shelve the next book automatically?

That is retention — not marketing luck

The Year-One Retention Milestones

Your actual benchmarks are not social media metrics.

They are:
[ ] 50+ reviews across all platforms
[ ] 100+ newsletter subscribers
[ ] 10+ repeat ARC readers
[ ] 5+ library placements
[ ] 3+ indie bookstore relationships
[ ] 1 signed preorder anchor for Book Two
[ ] 1 event (physical or digital) per quarter

If you hit those seven, you have traction.
You can build almost anything from traction.

ARC to Review Planner

ARC Window Dates: _____

ARC Team Goal (# of readers): _____

Review Hub URL: _____

Primary Review Platforms (circle 3–4):

Amazon / Goodreads / B&N / Kobo / StoryGraph / Website

Newsletter Conversion Targets

Subscriber Goal by Launch: _____

Post-Launch Growth Goal (90 Days): _____

Lead Magnet / Incentive: _____

End Of Chapter Checklist:

You are ready when:

[ ] Your Review Hub exists and works

[ ] ARC readers know where to leave reviews

[ ] Newsletter subscription is positioned BEFORE Amazon

[ ] QR codes link to your website, not retailers

[ ] You can repeat this process without rewriting it

If not, pause.

Fix the system.

Then proceed.

Chapter Ten

Momentum, Monetization, and the Long Game

From One Book to a Career

B Y NOW, YOU HAVE built the essential infrastructure most self-published authors never reach. This final chapter exists for one purpose. To prevent you from stopping here.

Because one of the most dangerous misconceptions in publishing is this:
"Once the book is out, the work is done."

You now have:
- A website you own
- ISBNs you control (or a publisher manages consistently)
- Metadata and BISAC that actually match reality
- Search signals established across SEO and AI-SEO
- ARC readers, reviews, and early credibility
- The beginnings of bookstore, library, and local community presence

Once the book is out, the *marketing* begins.
Once readers arrive, the *career* begins.
Once systems run, the *future* begins.

The First-Year Mindset Shift

A single book is a product.
A second book is a pattern.
A third book is a career.

Readers trust momentum.
Retailers trust consistency.
Libraries trust series.
Algorithms trust proof.

<u>Your job over the next 12 months is to prove you are continuing — and to do it visibly.</u>

Do that, and every action becomes more efficient:
• Each new book lifts the backlist
• Reviews compound
• Libraries and bookstores reorder on expectation
• SEO expands without rebuilding
• Readers begin arriving on purpose

Momentum is not loud.
It is consistent.

Your 12-Month Continuity Plan

This is not a checklist of tasks. It is your path for progression.

Months 1–3 (Post-Launch Stabilization)
• Maintain ARC engagement (respond, thank, update)
• Add 5–10 new backlinks from credible sources
• Conduct a metadata audit (ISBN, BISAC, pricing, keywords)
• Attend at least one physical event — bookstore, library, or community

Months 4–6 (Expansion & Proof of Life)
• Draft or outline Book Two
• Announce that Book Two exists (even if it's early)
• Revisit indie bookstores that carried Book One
• Pitch one workshop or library event
• Add a character teaser, prologue, or excerpt to your website

Months 7–9 (Series Identity)
• Create a unified series banner or tagline
• Add cross-book advertising ("If you enjoyed this...")
• Update Amazon/Goodreads/Google Books with series info
• Prepare Book Two preorder window or announcement

Months 10–12 (Positioning for Next Release)
• Finalize metadata for Book Two early
• Schedule ARC period for Book Two
• Begin pre-orders (2–3 months out)
• Restart bookstore/library contact with updated materials
• Re-run your email list with renewed value, not repetition

Outcome of 12 months:
Your next launch is not a restart — it is a continuation.

Monetization Over The Life Of Your Book

There are five forms of revenue in a modern author career, over the life of their book. Most authors only use one:

1. **Direct sales** (highest profit)

2. **Retail sales** (credibility + discoverability)

3. **Libraries & institutions** (longevity + readership)

4. **Events & appearances** (connection + authority)

5. **Future rights** (translation, audio, foreign markets)

At this stage, do not chase all five at once.

Focus on:
• Direct + Retail + Libraries
If these three work, everything else has a runway.
If they don't, translation rights and foreign editions won't matter yet.

Future rights are not the goal of Book One — they are enabled by the performance of Book One.

Protecting Your Infrastructure

Most authors fail here — not because of laziness, but because of drift.

To prevent drift, review quarterly:
• ISBN alignment across platforms
• BISAC accuracy and category shifts
• Amazon/Ingram metadata consistency
• Website links, load speed, and store function
• Library and bookstore reorder paths
• Review growth vs. stagnation
• Newsletter health (new subscribers vs. dead weight)
• Time spent vs. return earned

Your system should not stay still.
It should stay aligned.

Three Professional Signs That You Are A Serious Author

There are three signals that tell the industry you are not a hobbyist:

1. A website you own
Not a Linktree, not a social profile — a place you control.

2. ISBNs you control (or a publisher manages for you)
Free ISBNs scatter identity across systems. Controlled ISBNs anchor it.

3. BISAC and metadata chosen with intent, not convenience
These are not clerical fields. These determine visibility.

If these three are right, everything else becomes easier.

If any one of them is wrong, everything else becomes harder.

This book was written to prevent that.

Chapter Eleven

Publishing Isn't Marketing

Marketing Is a System You Build Once and Refine Forever

Y OU CAN FINISH THIS book in a weekend.
You will build the system it describes over months.

You will refine it over years.

And somewhere in that stretch of time, a reader who has never met you will pick up your book, buy it without hesitation, and tell someone else.

Not because you asked them to.

Because the system you built led them there.

This is what separates hopeful publishing from professional publishing.

In a marketplace where millions of books arrive every year, where search engines index at scale, where AI recommends based on trust signals, where bookstores ration shelf space, where libraries catalog selectively, and where readers are overwhelmed with choice —
you cannot rely on luck.

You rely on infrastructure.

A website you own.

ISBNs you control.

Metadata that matches reality.

A review strategy that creates confidence.

A release pattern that builds readership.

A system that compounds.

If you build that, you are no longer marketing a book.

You are establishing a presence.

The bookstore shelf stops being a lottery.

It becomes an address.

A location readers can return to.

A reminder that you are still here.

Still writing.

Still worth finding.

You are left with these parting thoughts:

Publishing is the moment your book enters the world.

Marketing is how the world finds its way back to you.

Build the system once.

Maintain it forever.

Grow with every title.

Your readers are waiting.
Now you know how to help them find you.

***

Many authors feel frustrated when a reader does not leave a review. This is the moment when you understand that moment as they feel it. If you enjoyed this book, please visit the website for links to leave a review:

***

https://markwilderauthor.com/publishing_isnt_marketing/

About the author

M ARK WILDER HAS WORKED in marketing for more than 30 years, beginning in the early days of digital and social media with platforms such as Yahoo, Craigslist, and MySpace. Long before online marketing became standardized, his focus was on how people actually discover information, evaluate credibility, and decide what to trust.

He holds a Bachelor of Science in Marketing with a concentration in Social Media Marketing from Southern New Hampshire University and has coordinated high-value marketing campaigns in major U.S. markets, including San Francisco and San Jose, California.

He is the author of four books and brings a practitioner's perspective to the realities of visibility, discoverability, and audience-building in modern publishing. After repeatedly encountering new authors who were unaware of critical structural pitfalls in self-publishing — from metadata errors to platform dependency and loss of control — he founded an author-centric publishing house designed to provide professional publishing infrastructure at roughly the same cost authors often pay to navigate the process alone.

This book was written to make those hidden pitfalls visible. It is not a promotional guide, but a practical framework to help authors understand how publishing systems actually work, how marketing decisions compound over time, and how to build a sustainable career rather than chase short-term exposure.

He has lived and worked across the United States, Europe, Australia, and the Caribbean, experiences that inform both his writing and his approach to publishing in a global marketplace.

Also By Mark Wilder

I Was Never Supposed To Exist — But I Do
Memoir — Chantelle

<u>Flying Dutchman Series</u>
2 A.M.
Flashpoint Zero
<u>If I Had A Genie</u>
The Pact of Stars and Stone
Nonfiction / Reference
<u>The Wilder Way to Getting Things Done</u>
<u>Reference Books to Improve Your Life</u>
Publishing Isn't Marketing
Is Your Novel "Just Another Can Of Beans" On The Shelf?
Publishing Isn't Marketing Companion Workbook
Is Your Novel "Just Another Can Of Beans" On The Shelf?

COMING IN 2026

Nonfiction / Reference
<u>The Wilder Way to Getting Things Done</u>
<u>Reference Books to Improve Your Life</u>
The 96-Hour Rule
Keep Projects Moving, Hit Your Deadlines, Finish What You Start
The 96-Hour Rule Quarterly Workbook
Keep Projects Moving, Hit Your Deadlines, Finish What You Start
<u>Historical Collections</u>
History's Greatest Battle Poems
A Collection of the World's Greatest Battle Poems Through 1930
Fiction
<u>Flying Dutchman Series</u>
The Architect — Cathedral of the World
<u>The Guardian Chronicles</u>
The Crimson Petal and the Blade
<u>The Viking Queens — A Three-Era Saga</u>
<u>Era I — Rise & Consolidation</u>
Åsa of Agder (Norway)
Thyra "Danebod" (Denmark)
Ragnhild Sigurdsdotter (Norway)
Gyda Eiriksdottir (Norway)
Please visit:
MarkWilderAuthor.com

www.ingramcontent.com/pod-product-compliance
Lightning Source LLC
Chambersburg PA
CBHW042347030426
42335CB00031B/3486